# The Best 50
# MARGARITAS

## Dona Z. Meilach

BRISTOL PUBLISHING ENTERPRISES
San Leandro, California

Printed in the United States of America.

ISBN: 1-55867-272-9

| | |
|---|---|
| Cover design: | Frank J. Paredes |
| Cover photography: | John A. Benson |
| Food stylist: | Susan Devaty |
| Illustration: | Hannah Suhr |

# MARGARITAS AND TEQUILA

Margaritas are among today's most fashionable cocktails, thanks to the increasing popularity of tequila. New trends in drinking and greater promotion of tequila by producers and distributors have helped to generate interest in the Mexican-produced liquor. The result is that margaritas, traditionally made with a tequila base, have become trendier than ever. There are new types of tequila, with different producers introducing fresh flavors and new brands. Bartenders and aficionados of the drink have gone beyond traditional mixtures of tequila, Triple Sec or Cointreau and lime juice. They are adding flavored liqueurs, fruits and other spirits to the basic margarita and — caramba — in just a few years, an infinite number of margarita recipes have appeared.

Caramba indeed! The margarita originated in Mexico and its history is steeped in fascinating lore. There are different stories regarding its origin. Some historians believe that the drink was named for Marjorie King, a Hollywood actress during the prohibition days of the 1920s. Ms. King would whisk down to Tijuana for an occasional cocktail and stay at a favorite Tijuana ranch; the admiring owner named the drink after her. Another popular story is that it was invented in 1948 when Margarita Sames, who lived in Acapulco, Mexico, mixed her two favorite spirits, tequila and Cointreau. Her loving husband had her named etched onto a glass and thus was born the Margarita. No doubt there are other stories, but these predominate.

Regardless of the drink's namesake, today it ranks in popularity with the martini, gin and tonic and Tom Collins. Margarita lovers and their preferred concoctions are as varied as the drinkers themselves. It seems that each bartender and each person who mixes a margarita at home has his or her special combination of ingredients and mixing methods. It's not easy to go far wrong; the only thing that will make a margarita really bad is using poor quality tequila (it can taste like gasoline), reconstituted lime juice or dreadful sweet and sour mixes. Bad ingredients result in bad drinks; high quality ingredients, properly blended, make the finest drinks.

The recipes in this book will result in great-tasting margaritas. Tastes differ, along with the type of tequila used. The nonprofessional drink mixer should play with the ingredients. Each person likes to perfect a special margarita recipe. Even bartenders become known for their margaritas. On the Internet, you can find restaurants rated for the quality of their margaritas: good, fair and poor.

## INGREDIENTS

A margarita generally consists of about 1 1/2 ounces tequila, 1/2 ounce Triple Sec, 1/2 ounce lime juice, 1/2 ounce of a selected mix and ice. A specially shaped margarita glass, its rim frosted with salt, is the preferred serving container, but tumblers, highball glasses, old-fashioned glasses and wine glasses are all used. Rims may be unfrosted or frosted with salt or sugar.

Tequila is usually the base ingredient. Occasionally, rum or vodka may be used instead of tequila.

The second ingredient enhances the taste of the base and adds color to the drink; it may be Triple Sec, Cointreau, blue curaçao, peach, strawberry or another liqueur.

The third ingredient flavors the drink and adds to the aroma; it may be a fruit juice such as lemon, lime or orange, or a sweet and sour mix composed of lemon and lime.

Ice is used to chill the drink and dilute its alcoholic strength.

## TEQUILA

Tequila is an alcoholic drink made from juice from the heart of the agave plant that grows in the arid highlands of central Mexico. This juice is mixed with pulque, a fermented by-product of the agave juice, for about two and a half days. The mix is then double-distilled, producing clear, white tequila.

The agave plant is a succulent, not a cactus. Its name comes from the Greek word for "noble" and it is indeed a noble plant. A mature agave has leaves 5 to 8 feet tall and 7 to 12 feet in diameter, with a lifespan of 8 to 15 years. Only the blue agave, the *Tequilana Weber*, may be used in tequila production. There are probably over 600 varieties. Just as wines can differ by grapes grown on different parts of a hillside, agave plants, too, yield differences in taste depending on how and where they are grown and what other plants grow nearby. Some have a fruitier flavor than others. The taste differences between tequilas may be likened to those between Scotch and rye whiskeys, or between cognac and brandy.

About 125 years ago, distillers around the town of Tequila, in the central state of Jalisco, Mexico, began producing a mezcal using the whole heart of the blue agave indigenous to the region, instead of other agave varieties used in mezcal production. Today, the Mexican government has set standards for tequila similar to French laws governing cognac. Tequila can only be made from one species of the blue agave grown mainly in the state of Jalisco and only a few other areas nearby.

Some people confuse tequila with the popular Mexican drink, mezcal. Tequila is a type of mezcal, but mezcals are not tequilas. Tequila is double- or triple-distilled. Mezcal is usually distilled only once. Tequila and mezcal are similar in alcohol content (around 38% to 40%), though mezcal tends to be a little stronger.

Prices for tequila vary according to quality, amount of aging and agave content. A 100% agave content is preferred, and if the bottle isn't marked as such, it probably isn't. Inexpensive tequilas are usually not 100% agave.

## TYPES OF TEQUILA

There are basically four varieties of tequila. Try different types and then decide which you prefer.

**Blanco** or **plata** (white or silver) is the most common. It is stored less than 6 days and is called "unaged." It is tasty and robust with a distinct fresh, fruity, agave flavor.

**Joven** or **abocado** is smoother than blanco; may also be labeled "gold"; is basically the same as blanco, but artificially colored to make it appear aged.

**Tequila reposado** (means rested) is aged in wood barrels for a minimum of 60 days. The wood alters the flavor and lightly modifies the color. Reposado has a light, mellow, peppery flavor and a pale straw color.

**Añejo** (aged or vintage) is tequila that has been aged in government-sealed barrels for a minimum of a year and perhaps as long as five years. It may have a smoother taste than white and a soft golden color. Some have a woody aroma but much of the taste differences are also due to production factors. Premium tequila is aged in oak casks for up to four years. Gold tequila, aged for about five years, gets its rich color from the influence of the barrel. It is not artificially colored like the unaged tequila.

Tequilas may be labeled white, silver, gold, aged, premium, super premium and by brand names such as Jose Cuervo, Herradura, Sauza Conmemorativo, Sauza Hornitos, Patron and so forth. Margarita aficionados know the taste and feel the difference as they sip different tequilas. For some people, almost any tequila will work in a margarita because the other ingredients imbue much of the flavor. However, the best tequilas will result in better-tasting drinks.

Many liquor stores carry miniature bottles of the different kinds so you can become familiar with them without investing in an entire bottle. Some brands have small bottles of each type in one package so you can become familiar with the flavor differences economically.

## TRIPLE SEC, COINTREAU, GRAND MARNIER

Triple Sec, Cointreau and Grand Marnier are liqueurs most often used as the flavor-producing ingredient in a margarita. These liqueurs lend an orange flavor to the drink. One might think *Triple Sec* means triple-dry, but in this case it means triple-distilled. Blue curaçao is another orange-flavored drink used to add flavor as well as a blue color to margarita drinks. Other flavored liqueurs are used either in conjunction with an orange-flavored liqueur or by themselves.

## JUICES AND FRUITS

Lemon and lime juice are essential ingredients of the margarita. When fresh juices or fruits are not available, reconstituted and frozen products may be used, but their taste is not equal to fresh.

## SWEET AND SOUR MIXES

Prepared sweet and sour mixes and other margarita mixes vary in composition and in quality. Some are made of sugar and lime or lemon, some contain fruit juices, and some have alcohol such as Triple Sec. A mix is easier to incorporate in cold drinks than sugar, which doesn't dissolve readily. Refrigerate after opening a prepared bottle of mix, or after cooling a homemade recipe. When buying prepared margarita mixes, read labels carefully; some contain tequila and are ready to serve. Some resemble a homemade sweet and sour mix. Some are labeled sweet and sour mix but have the same ingredients as margarita mix.

## SWEET AND SOUR MIX

*Here's a homemade sweet and sour mix recipe. You can vary the proportions to suit your taste. This recipe calls for a sweet-sour ratio of 1:1 (1 cup sugar to 1 cup lemon-lime juice), but the ratio can be adjusted according to your taste.*

| | |
|---|---|
| 1 cup water | ½ cup fresh lemon juice |
| 1 cup sugar | ½ cup fresh lime juice |

Combine water and sugar in a large saucepan. Stir over medium heat until sugar dissolves. Bring to a boil and cool. Add lemon and lime juices and chill until cold. Cover and keep refrigerated for about 1 month. Makes 2 cups.

## FROSTING THE RIM OF THE GLASS

Traditionally, the rim of a margarita glass is frosted with salt or sugar. There are different ways to frost the rim of a glass using kosher salt, a special margarita salt, table salt or sugar. Kosher salt is coarse and makes a nice edge on the glass; table salt tends to clump up. Margarita salt has a texture between the two and is probably the optimum to use. Superfine sugar or other sugar may be used also.

If the drink uses a citrus fruit garnish such as a lemon, lime or orange wedge, rub a wedge of the fruit around the rim of the glass to moisten it before pouring the drink. While the rim is wet, dip the rim into a shallow saucer of salt or superfine sugar. The rim can also be moistened with fruit juice or whatever is used as the mix for the drink.

Dip the glass in water and then put it in the freezer for half an hour or so. Metal and silver mugs and cups will frost better than glass and plastic containers.

Some people will prefer their drink without a frosted rim.

Granulated sugar crystallizes and remains hard on the rim. Colored sugar adds to the appearance of the drink and is spectacular if used with a particular season. For instance, red or green sugar may be used at Christmastime, red sugar with a blue curaçao Margarita on Memorial or Flag Day.

**Note:** Metal and silver mugs and cups frost better than glass. Plastic will not frost when using lime or lemon juice. Instead, wet the rim with Rose's Lime Juice and then dip the rim of the glass into salt. Salt will not adhere to plastic if only fresh fruit is used.

## ICE

Ice is an essential ingredient of a margarita. Using crushed ice will make the drink slushy and result in a "frozen" margarita, which tends to dilute quickly. An option is to mix the drink without ice in a blender or shaker, put cubes into a 10- or 12-ounce tumbler and then pour the margarita over the ice.

For a large party, fill a tub with cracked ice, keep the glasses in the ice and use them as needed.

Always use freshly made ice cubes from clean ice trays.

For crushed or broken ice, use an electric ice crusher or a blender, or wrap cubes in a towel and hit them with a mallet.

The larger the piece of ice, the more slowly it will melt. Crushed ice melts the fastest, shaved or cracked ice second and cubes the slowest.

To make cracked ice, put several ice cubes in a towel or plastic bag and hit them with a hammer.

Always put the ice in a glass first and then add the liquid.

To measure for a frozen margarita, put ice and the ingredients in a glass, fill to the rim and then pour the contents into the blender. When blended, it will be exactly the right amount of liquid to fill the glass.

## GLASSES AND GARNISHES

Special stemmed margarita glasses or cocktail glasses may have either a rounded bowl, a V-shaped bowl, or a stepped bowl (smaller on the bottom and wider on the top). Glasses usually hold from $3\frac{1}{2}$ to 6 ounces. Larger margarita glasses may hold 10, 12 or 14 ounces of liquid. Margaritas may also be served in a tall rocks glass, a tumbler, an old-fashioned glass or a 5- or 6-ounce highball glass.

Salt or sugar frosting is the primary garnish, but drinks may also be decorated with lemon and lime slices propped on the edge of the glass. Pineapple cubes may be placed on a cocktail pick to garnish a pineapple margarita, a peach slice on a peach drink, a strawberry on a strawberry drink, a watermelon wedge in a watermelon drink etc. Sprigs of mint or other leaves add color. Cocktail straws are decorative and enhance the enjoyment of the drink for sipping. A variety of cocktail decorations is easily available.

## PREMIXED PRODUCTS

Among the premixed products now available are:

**Sour mix**  usually has lemon or lime

**Sweet and sour mix**  a mixture of sugar with lemon or lime

**Rose's Lime Juice** and **Rose's Lemon Juice**  smooth-tasting sweetened fruit juice mixtures

**Margarita mix**  similar to sweet and sour mix but with some flavoring added, usually lime, Triple Sec or orange

**Ready to Drink Margarita mix** (called RTD)  Just pour over ice and serve. These come in different fruit flavors such as strawberry, lime, mango and others. They usually contain gold tequila.

**Powdered mix in a pail**  You add the tequila, put it in the freezer for a few hours, than scoop it out to serve. It can be poured into a punch bowl so guests can ladle their drinks into a glass.

## STIRRING

To make a stirred margarita, put the ice in the mixing container, then add the remaining ingredients. Use a long bar spoon to stir it just enough to mix the ingredients, usually about 10 to 12 stirs. Stirring the drink too long tends to dilute the liquor. Strain out the ice using a bar strainer when you pour it into the serving glass. The glass may be chilled or ice added.

## SHAKING

Shakers are made of metal, glass or plastic. First, put the ice in the bottom part of the shaker and then add the other ingredients. Secure the lid on the shaker and shake vigorously forward and backward over your shoulder until the shaker feels cold, about 10 times. Too long a shake will dilute the drink. Separate the two halves of the shaker, lay a strainer over the bottom half and strain the drink into the serving glass.

## BLENDING

An electric blender is ideal for making frozen margaritas and for putting froth on drinks. Do not over-blend; rather pulse the liquid using four or five short bursts of the blender, so as not to create a slush of ice.

## FLOATING

A few recipes call for "floating" liquor on top of the drink. Floating keeps each ingredient in separate layers and is often referred to as layering. To float one liquor onto another, use a demitasse spoon. Hold it over, or in, the glass and slowly trickle the ingredient down over the back of the spoon into the drink.

## TOOLS

Having the right tools makes drink-mixing a pleasurable experience.

measuring jigger

shaker

strainer

bar glass

bar spoon

ice bucket

tongs

blender

bottle opener

corkscrew

pitcher

pourers

paring knife

muddler

cutting board and knife

juice squeezer

straws

wiping cloths or sponges

coasters

glasses, assorted

## HANDY MEASUREMENTS

| | | |
|---|---|---|
| 1 large jigger | = | 2 oz. |
| 1 jigger | = | 1½ oz. |
| 1 pony | = | 1 oz. |
| 1 tbs. | = | 3 tsp. |
| 1 cup (liquid) | = | 8 oz. |
| 2 cups | = | 1 pint |
| 1 fifth bottle liquor | = | ⅕ gallon or 25.5 oz. |
| 1 quart bottle | = | 32 oz. |
| 1 liter | = | 33.8 oz. |
| 750 milliliters | = | 25.5 oz. or 1 fifth |
| splash or spritz | = | a quick squirt from the bottle |

**Note:** A recipe that serves one will produce 3½ to 5 ounces of the margarita drink; it will vary according to the amount of ice and other ingredients used. Some recipes are offered to serve four or six people, or a crowd, but will still figure about 4 ounces per drink.

**CAUTION**

Most of these drinks have high alcohol content. Drinking too many margaritas can produce a hangover. Pregnant women are cautioned against consuming alcoholic drinks entirely. Do not drink and drive. Do not ride with someone who has been drinking and is driving. Alcohol cannot be consumed with many over-the-counter and prescription drugs.

# BASIC MARGARITA #1

*All ingredients in this basic recipe are equal amounts so increasing quantities for a crowd is very simple. Frosting the glasses is optional, depending on time constraints and the number of people to be served.*

1 oz. white tequila
1 oz. Triple Sec
1 oz. frozen orange juice concentrate
1 oz. fresh lime juice
1 tsp. superfine sugar

Add all ingredients to a shaker half-filled with ice and shake. Strain ingredients into a chilled cocktail glass.
Makes 1.

# BASIC MARGARITA #2

*There are probably as many "basic margarita" recipes as there are those who consider themselves authorities on the drink. Some of the factors which make a difference are: the type and brand of tequila used; whether the lime flavoring is reconstituted or fresh; and the method of mixing, icing and serving.*

| | |
|---|---|
| 1 wedge lime | ¾ oz. Triple Sec or Cointreau |
| salt | 2 oz. sweet and sour mix |
| ice cubes | 1 oz. fresh lime juice |
| 1½ oz. tequila | 1 wedge lime for garnish |

To frost the glass, rub lime wedge around the rim and dip rim in a saucer of salt. Put ice in a shaker and add tequila, Triple Sec, sweet and sour mix and lime juice. Shake. Serve in frosted glass. Add ice, if desired. Garnish with another lime wedge.

Makes 1.

## BASIC MARGARITA #2 — FROZEN

*Most margarita recipes can be made "frozen" with crushed ice as an alternative to "on the rocks" over ice cubes. This is the frozen version of* Basic Margarita #2.

| | |
|---|---|
| 1 wedge lime | ³/₄ oz. Triple Sec or Cointreau |
| salt | 3 oz. sweet and sour mix |
| ice cubes | 1¹/₂ oz. fresh lime juice |
| 1¹/₂ oz. tequila | 1 wedge lime for garnish |

To frost the glass, rub lime wedge around the rim and dip rim in a saucer of salt. Put crushed ice in a blender container and add tequila, Triple Sec, sweet and sour mix and lime juice. Shake. Serve in frosted glass. Garnish with another lime wedge.
Makes 1.

# BASIC MARGARITA #3

*This basic recipe calls for Rose's Lime Juice, which can be purchased at supermarkets or liquor stores. When you sip this drink, first you will taste the sweetness and then the acid from the lime juice, followed by the mellow taste of the tequila.*

$2/3$ cup tequila
$1/3$ cup Cointreau or Triple Sec
$1/4$ cup Rose's Lime Juice
juice of 1 fresh lime

Fill a shaker about $1/2$ full with ice cubes. Add tequila, Cointreau, Rose's and fresh lime juice and shake until cubes have diminished to about $1/2$ their original size. Strain and serve over ice. Use frosted glasses, if desired.

Makes 3 to 4.

# BASIC MARGARITA #4

*Most recipes call for ice cubes; this one begins with crushed ice. The crushed ice melts quickly so that the drink, which is strong initially, loses its wallop as you linger over it.*

3 cups cracked ice, divided
2 cups tequila
1 cup Triple Sec
1/2 cup freshly squeezed lime juice

Place one cup of the ice in a shaker. Add tequila, Triple Sec and fresh lime juice and shake. Divide remaining ice among 6 cocktail glasses and pour margaritas over.
Makes 6.

### VARIATION: BASIC MARGARITA #4 – FROZEN
Put all ice in the shaker with the liquid ingredients and shake until slushy. Serve in 6 cocktail glasses.

# BLENDED FROZEN MARGARITA

*This quick-to-prepare margarita will win accolades from your guests. Whip it up quickly in a blender container and serve it in stemmed cocktail or highball glasses. Add a lemon wheel over the edge and a straw for sipping and you'll win bartender stars.*

4 oz. frozen limeade concentrate
4 oz. tequila
2 oz. Triple Sec
about 2 cups ice cubes
orange or lime slices for garnish

Place frozen limeade concentrate in a blender container. Add tequila and Triple Sec. Blend, adding ice cubes, until mixture becomes slushy and holds peaks. Serve in chilled, stemmed margarita glasses with a lime or orange slices for garnish.

Makes 3 to 4.

# STIRRED FROZEN MARGARITA

*Using crushed ice will result in a slushy drink that is nice for sipping through a straw. Drinking it directly from the glass may chill the roof of the mouth and produce a temporary headache.*

2 wedges lime
salt or superfine sugar
6 oz. frozen limeade
  concentrate
6 oz. tequila

2 oz. Triple Sec
6 oz. lemon-lime soda
5 cups crushed ice
lime slices for garnish

To frost the glasses, rub lime wedges around the rims and dip rims in a saucer of salt or superfine sugar. Pour limeade concentrate, tequila, Triple Sec and soda into a large pitcher and stir to mix. Fill blender container with 5 cups crushed ice. Add drink mixture and blend until slushy. Pour into glasses and garnish with lime slices. Add cocktail straws for sipping.

Makes 6.

# BARTENDER'S FAVORITE MARGARITA

*A restaurant's reputation can be built on its patrons favoring a particular bartender's margarita-mixing skills. Many bartenders have their favorite combination of ingredients and mixing methods; or they may customize a mix with a particular type of tequila.*

| | |
|---|---|
| 1 wedge lime | 3 oz. fresh sweet and sour mix |
| salt | juice of 1/2 lime |
| ice cubes | 1 splash cranberry juice |
| 1 1/2 oz. premium tequila | 1/2 tsp. Grand Marnier |
| 3/4 oz. Triple Sec | 1 slice lime for garnish |

To frost the glass, rub lime wedge around the rim and dip rim in a saucer of salt. Put ice cubes in a shaker. Add tequila, Triple Sec, sweet and sour mix, lime juice and cranberry juice. Shake and strain into frosted cocktail glass. Float Grand Marnier on top. Garnish with lime wheel; add a straw and serve.

Makes 1.

# GOLD MARGARITA

*For a smooth, velvety tasting drink, use aged (añejo) gold tequila. This recipe serves 2 or allows a generous refill for one person. Use less tequila for a milder drink, or leave some crushed ice in the glass to dilute the drink.*

2 wedge lime
salt or superfine sugar
crushed ice cubes
2 oz. gold tequila

1/2 oz. Triple Sec or Cointreau
1 1/2 oz. commercially prepared
   margarita mix
2 dashes Rose's Lime Juice

To frost the glasses, rub lime wedges around the rims and dip rims in a saucer of salt or superfine sugar. Half fill a shaker with crushed ice and add tequila, Triple Sec, margarita mix and Rose's Lime Juice. Shake well and pour into a glass with some of the crushed ice.

Makes 2.

# MARGARITA ON THE ROCKS

*Many people believe that a good margarita must be shaken by hand rather than blended in a mixer. Use plenty of ice and shake until the ice cubes are about ½ their original size.*

1 wedge lime
salt
1½ oz. gold tequila
1½ oz. margarita mix
1–2 tbs. fresh lime juice
½ oz. Triple Sec

To frost the glass, rub lime wedge around the rim and dip rim in a saucer of salt. Place tequila, margarita mix, lime juice and Triple Sec in a large shaker with plenty of ice. Shake well and pour through a strainer into margarita glass.

Makes 1.

# MARGARITA PERFECTION

*The title "perfection" is given to many versions of the margarita. Each aficionado seems to have his or her own version of the "perfect" margarita and be passionate about it.*

3 wedges lime
1 1/2 oz. gold tequila
1/2 oz. white tequila
1 1/4 oz. Rose's Lime Juice
1/2 oz. Triple Sec
1 splash orange curaçao
crushed ice

Squeeze juice from 2 of the lime wedges into a shaker. Add tequilas, Rose's Lime Juice, Triple Sec and orange curaçao and shake well. Add fresh crushed ice to glass and strain mixture over ice into glass. Squeeze remaining lime wedge into glass.
Makes 1.

# PERFECT MARGARITA

*The combination of gold tequila and orange curaçao results in a beautifully colored, tasty drink. Some bartenders insist this is the real name and original recipe for this version of the* Margarita Perfection, *page 47.*

4 wedges lime
salt
crushed ice
2 oz. gold tequila
1/2 oz. white tequila

1 1/4 oz. Rose's Lime Juice
1/2 oz. Triple Sec
1 splash orange curaçao
crushed ice

With 2 of the lime wedges, moisten the rims of two cocktail glasses. Roll only outside edge of glasses in a saucer of salt. Place ice in the shaker and add remaining ingredients. Squeeze in juice of remaining 2 lime wedges. Shake well. Add fresh crushed ice to each glass and strain into glasses.

Makes 2.

# TOP SHELF MARGARITA

*This margarita looks dramatic when served in a tall wine glass. It's the quality of the tequila that makes it "top shelf." All top shelf recipes call for añejo or premium tequila.*

| | |
|---|---|
| 1 wedge lime | 1/4 oz. Cointreau |
| salt | 1 1/2 oz. margarita mix |
| ice cubes | 1 1/2 oz. water |
| 1 1/4 oz. premium tequila | lime wheel for garnish |
| 1/4 oz. Grand Marnier | |

To frost the glass, rub lime wedge around the rim and dip rim in a saucer of salt. Add ice to a blender container and then add tequila, Grand Marnier, Cointreau, margarita mix and water. Blend and pour into a tall wine glass. Garnish with a lime wheel on a cocktail pick.

Makes 1.

# ITALIAN (AMARETTO) MARGARITA

*Because almonds are grown in Italy and made into amaretto, this margarita is dubbed the "Italian Margarita." The amaretto mixed with the orange of the Cointreau is a pleasing-to-the-palate blend of flavors.*

1 oz. amaretto
1/2 oz. Cointreau
1/2 oz. tequila
2 oz. fresh lime juice
ice

Combine ingredients in a shaker with ice. Serve in a stemmed glass or on the rocks in a frosted glass. Garnish with a lime wedge.
Makes 1.

# PEACHY MARGARITA

*Peach margaritas take second place only to strawberry margaritas. Get the taste quickly with this easy recipe using peach schnapps for the peach flavor.*

1 oz. white tequila
1 oz. Triple Sec
1 oz. fresh lime juice
1 oz. peach schnapps
ice

Add all ingredients to a shaker half-filled with ice. Shake. Strain ingredients into a small cocktail glass with ice.
Makes 1.

# PEACH SCHNAPPS WITH CURAÇAO MARGARITA

*When fresh or canned peaches are not at hand, a bottle of peach schnapps will keep all your friends delighted, and the blue color of the curaçao will be a pleasant surprise.*

1 wedge lime
salt
1 oz. tequila
2 oz. peach schnapps

1 oz. blue curaçao
4 oz. sweet and sour mix
ice
1 wedge lime for garnish

To frost the glass, rub lime wedge around the rim and dip rim in a saucer of salt. Place tequila, schnapps, curaçao and sweet and sour mix in a shaker with ice. Shake and strain into a large, chilled margarita glass. Garnish with a lime wedge.
Makes 1.

# MOONLIGHT MARGARITA

*Ah, the color of blue curaçao! It can whisper many moods, and one is that of moonlight on a romantic evening.*

1 wedge lime
superfine sugar
1 oz. gold tequila
3 oz. margarita mix
$1/2$ cup crushed ice
1 splash blue curaçao
orange slice for garnish

To frost the glass, rub lime wedge around the rim and dip rim in a saucer of superfine sugar. Combine tequila, margarita mix, ice and curaçao and whip in a blender container until slushy and frothy. Garnish with orange slice and serve in frosted glass.

Makes 1.

# TURQUOISE MARGARITA

*Blue curaçao provides the jewel-like color and lime peel adds sharp freshness.*

| | |
|---|---|
| 6 wedges lime | ¼ cup blue curaçao |
| coarse salt | ½ lime, quartered |
| 1¼ cups margarita mix | 4 cups ice |
| ¾ cup tequila | lime slices for garnish |

To frost the glasses, rub lime wedges around the rims and dip rims in a saucer of salt. Combine margarita mix, tequila, curaçao and quartered lime in a blender container. Blend until lime is finely minced. Add ice and continue blending until the mixture is thick and smooth. Pour into glasses and garnish with lime slices.
Makes 6.

# BLUE MARGARITA

*Blue curaçao, made from the bitter peels of green oranges, originates from the Dutch West Indies. For greater drama, serve this as a single serving in an oversized margarita glass that holds 12 oz.*

1 wedge lime
salt
ice cubes
4 oz. sweet and sour mix
2 oz. tequila
½ oz. Triple Sec or Cointreau

½ oz. Grand Marnier
1 oz. blue curaçao
½ oz. orange juice
1 oz. lime juice
2 lime slices for garnish

Chill 2 margarita glasses. To frost the glasses, rub lime wedge around the rims and dip rims in a saucer of salt. Place ice cubes in a shaker. Add sweet and sour mix, tequila, Triple Sec or Cointreau, Grand Marnier, blue curaçao, orange and lime juice. Shake and strain into glasses. Garnish with lime wheels.

Makes 2.

# MARGARITA COOLER WITH CRÈME DE NOYA

*Crème de noya has a peach-apricot flavor and is one of many liqueurs that can be mixed with a basic margarita recipe to provide variety.*

1 oz. tequila
$\frac{1}{2}$ oz. Triple Sec
$\frac{1}{2}$ oz. crème de noya
$\frac{1}{4}$ oz. Rose's Lime Juice
2 oz. soda water
1 dash fresh lime juice

Half-fill a shaker with ice cubes. Add tequila, Triple Sec, crème de noya and Rose's Lime Juice. Shake and pour mixture and ice into a collins glass. Add soda and a dash of lime.
Makes 1.

# FROZEN MIDORI MARGARITA

*Midori is made from honeydew melon and has a distinctive melon taste and jewel-like green color. A lemon wheel garnish makes an appealing color contrast to the green liquid.*

1 oz. Midori liqueur
1½ oz. light rum
½ oz. Triple Sec
1 oz. sweet and sour mix
1 oz. lime juice
crushed ice

Combine Midori, rum, Triple Sec, sweet and sour mix and lime juice in a shaker with crushed ice and shake well. Pour into a bowl-shaped margarita glass. Makes 1.

# EMPEROR'S MARGARITA

*So-called because of the use of Mandarine Napoleon, a Belgian orange-flavored brandy made from cognac. It is flavored with essential oils extracted from fresh Sicilian tangerines and has an orangey flavor associated with margaritas. Mandarine Napoleon makes the drink different enough to elicit an eyebrow-raising taste-surprise. For a tropical variation, try adding 1/3 cup mango juice.*

1 oz. tequila
1 oz. Mandarine Napoleon or other orange-flavored liqueur
2 tsp. fresh lemon juice
1 dash curaçao
cracked ice

Combine tequila, Mandarine Napoleon, lemon juice and curaçao and stir gently. Fill an old-fashioned glass with cracked ice and pour mixture over.
Makes 1.

# HONEY MARGARITA

*A honey liqueur puts a new spin on a drink for those who like their margaritas sweet. Try serving it in a snifter glass instead of a traditional margarita glass and absorb the aroma.*

1 oz. white tequila
1 oz. Triple Sec
1 oz. fresh lime juice
1 oz. honey liqueur
ice

Add all ingredients to a shaker half-filled with ice and shake. Strain ingredients into a cocktail glass with some of the ice.
Makes 1.

# BLACKBERRY LIQUEUR MARGARITA

*Almost any flavored liqueur or syrup can be added to the recipe ingredients for a more distinctive taste and bouquet; in this case, blackberry is used. Try Midori (melon), crème de cassis (currants), crème de cacao (chocolate) or any other favorite taste.*

| | |
|---|---|
| ice cubes | 1 oz. fresh lime juice |
| 1 ½ oz. white tequila | 1 oz. blackberry liqueur |
| 1 oz. blue curaçao | |

Half fill a shaker with ice cubes. Add tequila, blue curaçao, lime juice and blackberry liqueur and shake. Strain ingredients into a chilled cocktail or highball glass.

Makes 1.

## VARIATION

Replace blue curaçao with Triple Sec or Cointreau. Serve in a frosted glass.

# RASPBERRY MARGARITA

*Chambord is a French liqueur with an intense flavor of black raspberries, fruits, herbs and honey. Its ruby red color and sweet taste complement the smoky taste of tequila. If Chambord is not available, any raspberry liqueur may be used. Use a thin glass so the color shows through.*

ice
1 1/2 oz. tequila
1/2 oz. Triple Sec
1/2 oz. Chambord raspberry liqueur
4 oz. lime juice or sour mix
wedge lime for garnish

Fill a shaker with ice. Add tequila, Triple Sec and raspberry liqueur and then add lime juice or sour mix. Shake and strain into a tumbler. Garnish with a lime wedge.

Makes 1.

# MARGARITA CRÈME DE FRAMBOISE

*When fresh raspberries aren't available, raspberry liqueur can be used for flavor and color. Serve in a frosted-rimmed glass or a high-ball glass.*

1½ oz. white tequila
1½ oz. Triple Sec
1 oz. fresh lime juice
1 oz. raspberry liqueur (crème de framboise)

Add tequila, Triple Sec, lime juice and raspberry liqueur to a shaker half-filled with ice. Shake. Strain ingredients into a cocktail glass with crushed ice.

Makes 1.

# WATERMELON AND STRAWBERRY MARGARITA

*This is very similar to the* Watermelon Margarita, *page 48, but the strawberries add body and variety to the flavor.*

1 ½ oz. tequila
¾ oz. Triple Sec
¾ oz. Midori melon liqueur
2 oz. sour mix
6 oz. cubed, seeded
  watermelon (about 1 cup)

3–4 strawberries
8 oz. ice
strawberries and watermelon
  wedges for garnish

Place all ingredients, except garnishes, in a blender container and blend. Serve in stemmed margarita glasses. Garnish each glass with a strawberry and a watermelon wedge.
Makes 2.

# WATERMELON MARGARITA

*The red color and sweet flavor result in a favorite refreshing summer drink. Garnish with a wedge of watermelon on a cocktail pick. The watermelon wedges may be frozen before using.*

2 wedges lime
superfine sugar
1½ oz. tequila
¾ oz. Triple Sec
¾ oz. Midori melon liqueur

2 oz. sour mix
6 oz. cubed, seeded
   watermelon (about 1 cup)
8 oz. ice
watermelon wedges for garnish

To frost the glasses, rub lime wedges around the rims and dip rims in a saucer of superfine sugar. Place tequila, Triple Sec, liqueur, sour mix, watermelon and ice in a blender container and blend. Garnish with watermelon wedges and serve in stemmed margarita glasses.

Makes 2.

# STRAWBERRY MARGARITA #1

*Fine sugar replaces salt for the frosted rim to result in a yummy drink that could easily serve as a dessert. Indulge lightly in this drink as the alcoholic content is high. This may also be served in a tall wine glass.*

1 wedge lime
superfine sugar
2 cups crushed ice
1½ oz. tequila

½ oz. Triple Sec
1 oz. lime juice
1 cup strawberries, fresh or
    frozen
lime slice for garnish

To frost the glass, rub lime wedge around the rim and dip rim in a saucer of superfine sugar. Place crushed ice, tequila, Triple Sec, lime juice and strawberries in a blender container. Blend well at high speed. Pour into sugar-rimmed glass and garnish with a lime slice to serve.

Makes 1.

# STRAWBERRY MARGARITA #2

*Diverse recipes for the same flavored drink can result in entirely different looks and tastes. With frozen strawberries and crushed ice blended, the result is closer to a frozen strawberry margarita. A sugar-frosted rim yields a sweeter taste than one frosted with salt.*

lime juice
superfine sugar
ice cubes
4–6 frozen strawberries
1 1/2 oz. gold tequila

1/2 oz. Triple Sec
1 oz. sweet and sour mix
1 scoop crushed ice
strawberry and lime wheel for
   garnish

To frost the glass, rub lime wedge around the rim and dip rim in a saucer of superfine sugar. Place ice cubes in a blender container and add strawberries, tequila, Triple Sec and sweet and sour mix. Shake well. Place crushed ice in glass and pour margarita over. Garnish with a strawberry and a lime wheel on a toothpick.

Makes 1.

# FRESH BLACKBERRY MARGARITA

*This recipe calls for blackberries, but blueberries, raspberries, strawberries or a combination may be used instead. The pink glow of the fruit results in a beautiful drink and adds a decorative touch to a luncheon table. Garnish with a lime wheel and a sprig of mint.*

2 cups (about 11 oz.) fresh blackberries
2 cups ice cubes
3/4 cup white tequila
1/2 cup fresh lime juice
1/4 cup sugar

Puree blackberries in a blender container. Force puree through a fine sieve into a small bowl and discard solids. Put ice in a cocktail shaker. Combine puree with tequila, lime juice and sugar in the cocktail shaker and shake well. Strain mixture into stemmed margarita glasses. Frost glasses, if desired.
Makes 4.

# FRESH RASPBERRY MARGARITA

*Fresh red raspberries change the color and taste of a basic margarita and produce a drink that could add color to a festive table. The raspberry flavor, combined with the orange in the Triple Sec, makes a delicious-tasting, fragrant fruity drink for a shower or luncheon.*

| | |
|---|---|
| lime juice | 1 1/4 oz. gold tequila |
| colored sugar (red is nice) | 1/2 oz. Triple Sec |
| ice | 1 oz. sweet and sour mix |
| 2 oz. frozen raspberries | lime wheel for garnish |

To frost the glass, rub lime wedge around the rim and dip rim in a saucer of colored sugar. Place raspberries, tequila, Triple Sec and sweet and sour mix in a blender container with ice. Blend until frothy. Garnish with a lime wheel.

Makes 1.

# STRAWBERRY-ORANGE MARGARITA

*This is a fresh variation on the popular strawberry margarita. Add more strawberry liqueur if desired.*

lime wedges
salt
ice cubes
1 1/4 oz. tequila
2 oz. margarita mix
1/2 oz. Grand Marnier

1 oz. strawberry liqueur (crème de fraises)
1 oz. orange juice
4 large strawberries
orange slice for garnish

To frost the glass, rub lime wedge around the rim and dip rim in a saucer of sugar. Place ice cubes in a blender and add tequila, margarita mix, Grand Marnier, strawberry liqueur, orange juice and strawberries. Blend well and pour into glass. Garnish with an orange slice.

Makes 1.

# CACTUS PEAR MARGARITA

*If you live where cactus grow, you can probably harvest these cactus pears yourself. Do this carefully and remove the needles. You can also buy cactus pears at the grocery store with the needles removed. To "muddle" means to crush the pear in the bottom of a bowl or cup with a wooden or metal stick with a bulb-like end.*

1 cactus pear, muddled  
1 scoop ice  
$1/2$ oz. silver tequila

$2/3$ oz. Cointreau  
juice of $1/2$ lime

Peel and slice pear. Muddle pear and squeeze out pulp. Put pulp in a shaker and add scoop of ice, tequila, Cointreau and lime juice. Shake sharply. Strain liquid from shaker into a cocktail or highball glass. Add any remaining pulp to glass.

Makes 1.

# CANTALOUPE MARGARITA

*Fresh cantaloupe yields a lovely yellow-gold color that is intensified when gold tequila is used.*

4 slices fresh cantaloupe
1/2 oz. gold tequila
1/2 oz. Cointreau
1/2 oz. melon liqueur
juice of 1/2 lemon
1 small scoop ice
lemon wheel for garnish

Place cantaloupe, tequila, Cointreau, melon liqueur and lemon in a blender container and blend until smooth. Place ice in a chilled cocktail glass and pour blended mixture over. Garnish with a lemon wheel on rim of glass and serve with a straw.

Makes 1.

# FROZEN HONEYDEW MARGARITA

*Take advantage of honeydews in season to make this refreshing rendition of a margarita. Frozen melon can be bought when honeydew melons are not in season.*

3½ cups cubed honeydew melon
¾ cup white tequila
⅓ cup fresh lime juice
2½ tbs. sugar, or to taste
4 mint sprigs, optional

Peel and seed honeydew melon. Cut fruit into ½-inch cubes. Freeze cubes in a plastic bag for at least 3 hours. Remove from plastic bag and puree in a blender container with tequila, lime juice and sugar until smooth. Pour into stemmed cocktail glasses. If desired, garnish with mint sprigs.

Makes 4.

# FROZEN PINEAPPLE MARGARITA

*In this recipe you may prefer to use ¹/₂ Triple Sec and ¹/₂ Grand Marnier for economy. Pineapple may be replaced or mixed with strawberry, peach, mango, nectarine or other fruit in season.*

5 wedges lime
salt
3 cups frozen pineapple chunks
2 cups tequila
1 cup Triple Sec or Grand
    Marnier

¹/₂ cup fresh squeezed lime
    juice
1 cup pineapple juice
ice cubes
unfrozen pineapple chunks for
    garnish

To frost the glasses, rub lime wedges around the rims and dip rims in a saucer of salt. Place frozen pineapple chunks in a large pitcher. Add tequila, Triple Sec, lime and pineapple juices. Add ice cubes, if desired. Stir well. Garnish each glass with a couple of unfrozen pineapple chunks on a toothpick.

Makes 8 to 10.

## GRAPEFRUIT MARGARITA
## (MARGARITAS DE TORONJA)

*Margaritas traditionally have an orange-lime citrus taste, but replace those with grapefruit for a distinctly altered flavor and taste sensation.*

8 grapefruit wedges
superfine sugar
2 cups ice
¾ cup grapefruit juice

6 oz. tequila
2 oz. Triple Sec
grapefruit wedges for garnish

To frost the glasses, rub grapefruit wedges around the rims and dip rims in a saucer of superfine sugar. Place ice in a blender container and add grapefruit juice, tequila and Triple Sec. Blend and pour into frosted glasses. Garnish each glass with a grapefruit wedge on the rim.

Makes 6 to 8.

# PEACH MARGARITA

*Serve this in a tall wine glass and garnish with a lime wheel and a peach slice. It's smooth but packs a divinely dangerous punch, so be careful.*

2 oz. canned peach slices with syrup
1 1/2 oz. gold tequila
1/2 oz. peach schnapps
1/2 oz. Triple Sec
1 oz. sweet and sour mix
1 scoop crushed ice
lime wheel and peach slice for garnish

Dip the glass rim into peach juice and then into superfine sugar. Place peach slices, tequila, schnapps, Triple Sec, sweet and sour mix and ice in a blender container and blend until frothy. Garnish with lime wheel and peach slice.

Makes 1.

# TROPICAL MARGARITA

*This unique combination of guava, papaya and coconut is a favorite at a Denver restaurant.*

6 wedges lime
superfine sugar
1½ cups sweet and sour mix
½ cup gold tequila
6 tbs. papaya nectar

6 tbs. guava nectar
¼ cup canned cream of
  coconut
8 ice cubes
6 lime slices for garnish

To frost the glasses, rub lime wedges around the rims and dip rims in a saucer of superfine sugar. Combine sweet and sour mix, tequila, nectars, coconut and ice cubes in a blender container and blend until smooth. Pour into glasses and garnish each with a lime slice.

Makes 6.

# PINK CADILLAC

*This rendition derives its name from the color imparted by the cranberry juice. The creator also believes it's a top-of-the-line drink, hence the name "Cadillac."*

1 wedge lime
superfine sugar
2 oz. tequila
1/2 oz. Cointreau

1/2 oz. Grand Marnier
3 oz. cranberry juice
1 oz. lime juice
1 wedge lime for garnish

To frost the glass, rub lime wedge around the rim and dip rim in a saucer of superfine sugar. Shake tequila, Cointreau, Grand Marnier, cranberry juice and lime juice with ice. Strain into sugar-rimmed glass and garnish with lime wedge.

Makes 1.

**VARIATION**

Omit cranberry juice to make it a plain Cadillac.

# FRESH ORANGE JUICE MARGARITA

*The bartender who uses this recipe insists that fresh orange juice produces a better tasting drink. Hearty shaking gives the drink a fluffy froth that is conducive to slow sipping.*

| | |
|---|---|
| 1 wedge lime | 1/2 oz. Grand Marnier |
| salt | 1/2 oz. fresh orange juice |
| 8 ice cubes | 1 oz. Rose's Lime Juice |
| 2 oz. gold tequila | 4 oz. sweet and sour mix |
| 1/2 oz. Cointreau | orange slices for garnish |

To frost the glass, rub lime wedge around the rim and dip rim in a saucer of salt. Put ice cubes in a shaker and add remaining ingredients, except orange slices. Shake well. Pour into 1 oversized cocktail glass or two regular-size glasses. Add orange slices for garnish.

Makes 1 or 2.

# MARGARITA WITH BEER #1

*Beer drinkers will enjoy this combination because it's delicious, different and fun to drink a margarita from a beer mug.*

2 wedges lime
salt
ice
1 1/2 oz. tequila
1/2 oz. Triple Sec
1 oz. lemon juice
9 oz. cold draft beer
splash of lime juice

To frost the beer glasses, rub lime wedges around the rims and dip rims in a saucer of salt. Put ice in a shaker and add other ingredients. Shake and strain into salt rimmed mugs.
Makes 2.

# MARGARITA WITH BEER #2

*There's a heightened zest in this recipe, thanks to the addition of beer.*

1 can (6 oz.) frozen limeade, undiluted
6 oz. tequila
3 oz. Triple Sec
1 heaping tsp. confectioners' sugar
3 oz. beer, optional
crushed ice

In a blender container, place limeade, tequila, Triple Sec and confectioners' sugar. Add beer, if desired, and process until well blended. Half-fill cocktail or highball glasses with crushed ice and pour mixture over.

Makes 4 if beer is used; without the beer, makes 3.

# MARGARITA WITH BEER #3

*Be creative with basic margarita recipes and feel free to add logical ingredients. The addition of beer in a margarita is gaining popularity. Some people prefer using beer that is flat rather than bubbly fresh.*

| | |
|---|---|
| 2 wedges lime | ice cubes |
| salt | 1/2 oz. orange juice |
| 6 oz. beer | 1 oz. lime juice |
| 1/2 oz. Grand Marnier | 4 oz. sweet and sour mix |
| 1/2 oz. Cointreau | orange slices for garnish |
| 2 oz. tequila | |

Chill a large margarita glass. To frost the glasses, rub lime wedges around the rims and dip rims in a saucer of salt. Place all ingredients except garnish in a shaker. Add ice cubes and shake well. Garnish glasses with an orange slice on the rim.

Makes 2.

# FROZEN ICE CREAM MARGARITA

*Häägen-Daz is a widely-available gourmet ice cream brand. Their Margarita Sorbet replaces the sweetness of the Cointreau or Triple Sec normally used, lowers the alcohol content of the drink and tastes like a spiked ice-cream shake.*

1 pint Häägen-Daz Margarita Sorbet
1 cup lime-flavored mineral water
2 oz. tequila, or to taste
crushed ice
lime wheels for garnish
cherries for garnish

Soften sorbet and place in a blender container. Add lime-flavored water and tequila and blend until smooth. Pour over crushed ice in glasses. Garnish each glass with a lime wheel and a cherry and add straws.

Makes 4.

# VODKA MARGARITA

*Only dyed-in-the-wool Triple Sec drinkers will miss its orange flavor in this recipe. Many people prefer vodka to the combination of tequila and Triple Sec because it has less acid content. A splash of orange juice and frosted glasses are optional.*

6 oz. frozen limeade
6 oz. vodka
6 oz. water
6 oz. ice
1 splash orange juice, optional

Place limeade, vodka and water in a blender container. Add ice and blend to consistency desired. Adding more ice or crushed ice will make it slushier. Serve in a margarita glass or on the rocks in a tumbler.

Makes 4.

## RUM AND LEMON MARGARITA

*The Bacardi® Rum Company offers this recipe using their Bacardi® Limón Rum instead of tequila as the main ingredient.*

| | |
|---|---|
| 1 wedge lime | 1 1/2 oz. Bacardi® Limón Rum |
| salt | 1/2 oz. Triple Sec |
| ice cubes | 1 oz. lime juice |

To frost the glass, rub lime wedge around the rim and dip rim in a saucer of salt. Place ice cubes in shaker and add rum, Triple Sec and lime juice. Shake vigorously and pour into margarita glass.
Makes 1.

### VARIATION
Replace Limón Rum with Bacardi® Carta Blanca light-dry rum.

# MARGARITAS FOR A CROWD

*Several companies market prepared mixes in a bucket, or in packets, ready to be mixed with tequila and put in a freezer. The alcohol prevents the contents from freezing solid so the liquid will be slushy, cold and ready to serve.*

| | |
|---|---|
| 1 qt. gold tequila | lime wheels for garnish, |
| 2 cups Triple Sec | optional |
| 1 qt. sweet and sour mix | 30 fresh wedges lime |
| 2 qt. prepared margarita mix | salt |
| ½ cup lime juice | |

Mix all liquids together in a large plastic freezer-ready container. Serve in highball glasses and garnish with lime wheels, or to frost the glasses, rub lime wedges around the rims and dip rims in a saucer of salt. Fill glasses with a scoop or a ladle so as not to ruin the frosted edge.

Makes 25 to 30.

# GRAND GOLD MARGARITA WITH BEER

*Here's a crowd-pleasing recipe that is easy on your budget. The addition of beer makes the drink more economical and gives it a lofty richness, but be careful because this combination can be potent. Don't let the drinkers drive. Frost the glasses, if desired.*

| | |
|---|---|
| ice cubes | 3 oz. Cointreau |
| 12 oz. sweet and sour mix | 3 oz. Grand Marnier |
| 6 oz. gold tequila | 1 bottle Corona beer |

Fill a blender container with ice cubes. Pour sweet and sour mix, tequila, Cointreau, Grand Marnier and beer into blender container. For frozen margaritas, fill blender container with ice cubes and blend until ice is crushed. For margaritas on the rocks, use less ice and blend until ingredients are thoroughly mixed. The beer will create a frothy texture for the margarita.

Makes 10 to 12.

# MARGARITA SPRITZER

*A spritzer is a mild version of a drink with low alcoholic content. The seltzer or club soda reduces the potency of this drink and imparts a bubbly texture.*

4 ice cubes
1½ oz. tequila
1 oz. fresh lime juice
1 oz. Triple Sec
chilled seltzer or club soda
1 lime slice for garnish

Put 4 ice cubes in a tall glass and add tequila, lime juice and Triple Sec. Fill glass with seltzer or club soda and stir. Garnish with lime slice.

Makes 1.

## VIRGIN MARGARITA

*The simulated margarita taste without alcohol content is perfect for a designated driver who wants to maintain a social appearance.*

2 lime wedges
superfine sugar
1 1/2 cups ice
1/2 cup margarita mix
1/2 cup fresh orange juice
1 tbs. Rose's Lime Juice or fresh lime juice

To frost the glasses, rub lime wedges around the rims and dip rims in a saucer of superfine sugar. Place ice in a blender container and add margarita mix, orange juice and lime juice. Blend on low for 10 seconds and then on high for a few seconds or until smooth. Serve in highball glasses or tumblers.

Makes 2.

# MOCK-ARITA

*If you have nondrinkers in a group, or children who want to pretend they are grown up, serve them a* Mock-arita *or a* Virgin Margarita, *page 72.*

2 oz. sweet and sour mix
1 splash lime juice
1 splash orange juice
1 wedge lime
superfine sugar
slice orange or lemon for garnish
maraschino cherry for garnish

Blend sweet and sour mix with fruit juices. To frost the glass, rub lime wedge around the rim and dip rim in a saucer of superfine sugar. Garnish with fruit slice and cherry. Serve with a sipping straw.

Makes 1.

# INDEX